New Vanguard • 35

M26/M46 Pershing Tank 1943–53

Steven J Zaloga • Illustrated by Tony Bryan and Jim Laurier

First published in Great Britain in 2000 by Osprey Publishing,
Midland House, West Way, Botley, Oxford OX2 0PH, UK
44-02 23rd St, Suite 219, Long Island City, NY 11101, USA
E-mail: info@ospreypublishing.com

Transferred to digital print on demand 2010

First published 2000
7th impression 2008

Printed and bound by PrintOnDemand-Worldwide.com, Peterborough, UK

A CIP catalog record for this book is available from the British Library

ISBN: 978 1 84176 202 9

Editor: Chris Wheatley
Design: Melissa Orrom Swan
Originated by Colourpath, London, UK

Author's note
The author is indebted to many people who assisted on this project, and in particular would like to thank the staff of the Patton
Museum at Ft. Knox, Kentucky, for use of their superb archive, and Charles Lemons for help in photographing their restored
M26 Pershing. Thanks also to the staff of the library, archive, and special collection branch of the US Army Military History
Institute at the US Army War College, Carlisle Barracks, Pennsylvania.

FOR A CATALOG OF ALL BOOKS PUBLISHED BY OSPREY
MILITARY AND AVIATION PLEASE CONTACT:

Osprey Direct, c/o Random House Distribution Center,
400 Hahn Road, Westminster, MD 21157
Email: uscustomerservice@ospreypublishing.com

Osprey Direct, The Book Service Ltd, Distribution Centre,
Colchester Road, Frating Green, Colchester, Essex, CO7 7DW
E-mail: customerservice@ospreypublishing.com

www.ospreypublishing.com

M26/M46 PERSHING TANK 1943–53

BACKGROUND

The M26 Pershing tank was the ancestor of America's Cold War main battle tanks, the Patton tank series. The Pershing saw combat in the closing months of World War II and became the backbone of the US tank force during the Korean War. One of the lingering controversies about the Pershing is why it was not put into service sooner. The standard US Army tank of 1944, the M4 Sherman medium tank, was clearly inadequate when facing newer German tanks such as the Panther, and the Pershing would have put the US Army on a more equal footing with the Wehrmacht in 1944. However, it did not enter service until after the great tank battles in Normandy and the Ardennes, and even then in very small numbers. Why was the Pershing so delayed, and would it have made a difference?

US Tank Design Policy

In 1942 the United States was producing three medium tanks. The M3 Medium tank was already in combat with British forces in North Africa, where it was better known by its British name, the Grant. The M4 Medium tank was replacing the M3 on the assembly lines and would see combat later in the year in North Africa, in British service at El Alamein. The M7 Light tank had grown in size and firepower to the point where it was reclassified as a medium tank. Production was begun in December 1942 but soon halted as its features were not sufficiently superior to the M4 Medium tank to justify two separate designs.

US Army medium tank design in 1942 was guided by US Army Ground Force (AGF) doctrine. Medium tanks were employed primarily in two types of formation – separate tank battalions and armored divisions. The separate tank battalions were used to provide support to infantry divisions, usually on the basis of one battalion per division. In this role medium tanks were used to overcome pillboxes and

Although intended for combat in World War II, the M26 and M46 tanks saw most of their combat action in Korea. Here, a pair of M26 Pershing tanks of Co.C, 1st Marine Tank Battalion take up firing positions on the Korean central front on March 1 1951. (USMC)

enemy defensive positions that could not be defeated easily by infantry alone. In the armored division the tanks were expected to be used as "cavalry", carrying out the exploitation of breakthroughs after the enemy main line of resistance had been ruptured by the infantry divisions.

In neither of these roles was the medium tank's main mission to deal with enemy tanks. Instead, specialized tank destroyer battalions, equipped with lightly armored vehicles fitted with more powerful guns than the tanks were to rebuff enemy attacks. The standard tank destroyer for most of the war, the M10 gun motor carriage, was a derivative of the M4A2 Medium tank, with a more lightly armored superstructure, an open-top turret, and a 3in. anti-tank gun. This doctrine did not rule out the possibility that US tanks would encounter enemy tanks on the battlefield. Indeed, the design requirements for the M4 Medium tank called for a versatile dual-purpose gun, able to fire both an effective anti-armor projectile and a powerful high-explosive projectile. Nevertheless, the AGF doctrine inevitably meant that US medium tanks were not optimized for tank fighting, and that most of the attention in the development of anti-tank guns was focused on the tank destroyer. No other major army in World War II accepted or practiced this type of armored doctrine, with the Germans, Soviets, and British relying primarily on their tanks to fight enemy tanks.

The other strong influence on tank development in 1942 were the policies of the AGF Development Division, which sanctioned new weapon design. The AGF had two primary criteria for a new weapon:

The M6 Heavy tank was an archaic and technologically flawed design that compared badly to contemporary European heavy tanks like the German Tiger I or Soviet KV-1. Although favored by Ordnance, the US Armored Force had no use for it and it was produced in small numbers and never deployed in combat. (MHI)

battle-need and battle-worthiness. "Battle-need" meant that the new equipment had to be essential, not merely desirable. This was a major policy of the head of the AGF, LtGen Lesley McNair. He was insistent that the Army should not be burdened with too many weapon types, since the US Army would be fighting thousands of miles away from the continental United States and could not afford to complicate its logistics. As a result, the US Army was unwilling to adopt a specialized tank with heavier armor for the infantry support role. "Battle-worthiness" meant that the design had to be capable of performing its intended function but be sufficiently rugged and reliable to withstand the rigors of combat service without excessive maintenance demands. These policies meant that the Army did not favor the development of new tanks unless they were perceived as being absolutely essential; the AGF was generally unwilling to sanction development until pressured into doing so by the combat arms based on battlefield experience. As we shall see, the main reason that the M26 Pershing did not replace the M4 Sherman sooner was that the US Army recognized much too late that a new tank was needed.

US Heavy Tank Design

The United States developed the heavily armored T14 Assault tank to satisfy a British requirement for an infantry support tank. Such a tank would have been better suited to the separate infantry tank battalions than the thinly armored M4 Sherman. However, the Army Ground Force (AGF) favored standardization on a single design and did not foresee the vulnerability of the Sherman to German anti-tank weapons in 1944. (Patton Museum)

When the M4 tank went into combat in 1942 it was widely regarded as an excellent blend of armor, firepower, and mobility. Its 75mm gun could defeat any of the existing German tanks including the PzKpfw IV, its armor was reasonably resistant to standard German anti-tank guns such as the 50mm Pak 38, and it had speed and cross-country ability comparable to German tanks and often better than existing British designs. In keeping with the AGF's "battle-worthiness" criterion, it proved to be an extremely rugged and reliable design. Although intended for use by the US armored divisions and the separate tank battalions, its features were more attuned to the armored division's requirements. Infantry officers would have preferred a tank with thicker armor, better able to stand up to enemy anti-tank guns, even if this meant lower speed. As a result, US Army Ordnance had been developing a heavy tank, the M6, which was standardized in February 1942. It could most charitably be described as thoroughly mediocre. Pre-war regulations had obliged the designers to restrict its width, and as a result it was a tall and ungainly design. Its automotive reliability was poor, and its 3in. gun, while superior to the 75mm gun on the M4 Medium tank in anti-armor penetration, was not sufficiently superior to justify fielding such a tank. Ordnance continued to tinker with

the M6 Heavy tank through much of 1943, even though it had little support from the combat branches.

Britain's tank doctrine differed markedly from that of the US and included a requirement for more heavily armored tanks for the infantry support role. Due to the Lend-Lease agreement, Ordnance began the design of the T14 Assault tank specifically to meet the British infantry needs. This had the same firepower as the M4 Medium tank but was fitted with 100mm frontal armor, twice as thick as that of the M4. A year later, in the fall of 1942, Ordnance began working on a comparable design for the US Army use which would also use thicker frontal armor. However, since the tank would be used for both the infantry support and exploitation roles, higher mobility was required, including a maximum road speed of 35 miles per hour. The hull design was intended to be more compact than that of the M4 Medium tank, and at least three different guns would be tested on the design, including an automatic 75mm gun, the 3in. gun used on the M10 tank destroyer and the M6 Heavy tank, and a new 76mm gun being developed for the M18 tank destroyer. The new tank was to be powered by the new 500 horsepower Ford V8 used on both the M4A3 Medium tank and on the T14 Assault tank.

The new design, called the T20, would employ a torque-converter fluid drive transmission similar to that of the M6 Heavy tank. The program was later expanded to include the T22, with mechanical transmission, and the T23, with an electric drive transmission. To further complicate matters, one of the prototypes, the T20E3, was authorized to employ new torsion bar suspension instead of the volute spring suspension so characteristic of US Ordnance design up to this time. Another significant difference between the new T20 series and the M4 Medium tank was in the powertrain layout. On the M4, the transmission was in the front of the tank, which necessitated the use of a drive shaft

The Armored Force wanted a tank with the mobility of the Sherman and the armor of the T14 Assault tank. The T20E3 shows the beginnings of the Pershing design, including its characteristic torsion bar suspension. In contrast to the related T22 and T23 designs, the T20 series used the torque-converter fluid drive transmission similar to that on the M6 Heavy tank. (Patton Museum)

down the center of the fighting compartment, forcing the turret to be mounted higher than it might otherwise have been. This led to a higher hull profile, greater hull volume, and more weight. By placing the transmission at the rear, the turret could be lowered further into the hull. The reduction in the silhouette of the tank made it possible to reduce the internal hull volume and to increase the armor thickness without a drastic increase in the overall weight of the tank. This had the added benefit of making the tank less conspicuous on the battlefield when frontally engaging enemy tanks.

Work on the T20, T22, and T23 took place through the spring of 1943. Of all the designs, the only one to receive serious consideration by

The T22E1 used a mechanical syncromesh transmission. Here it is seen with one of the experimental horizontal volute spring suspensions. This version served as a trials vehicle for a 75mm gun with automatic loader. (Patton Museum)

the AGF was the T23. Although it had some significant advantages over the M4 Medium tank, it had problems as well. The T23 employed an electric transmission, which added about 1.9 tons to the weight of the tank compared to more conventional alternatives. Electric drives had been tried on tanks since the French St. Chamond of World War I, and the Germans were experimenting with a similar system on their Elefant tank destroyer. The normal gasoline engine was connected to an electrical generator which sent current to the electric traction motors that powered the track. In theory, electric drive promised to transmit more of the power from the engine to the drive sprocket, but in practice, all of these designs proved troublesome and expensive.

In April 1943 the pilot model was shown to the leadership of the US Army, including the Army Chief of Staff, Gen George C. Marshall, the head of AGF, LtGen Lesley McNair, and the head of the Armored Force, LtGen Jacob Devers. The new M6 Heavy tank and M7 Medium tank had proven to be complete flops, clearing the way for a new tank design. Ordnance claimed that the T23 was ready for production even though testing had not even begun. There was in informal agreement that 250 T23 tanks would be built.

By the time work began in earnest on the T23E3 pilot, the US Army had engaged in its first major tank battles in North Africa. The defeat at Kasserine Pass in Tunisia in February 1943 was not attributed to poor tank design, but rather to the inexperience of US troops and combat commanders. During the Tunisian campaign, the US Army encountered the new German Tiger heavy tank for the first time. The Tiger was vastly more powerful than the M4 Medium tank, being capable of destroying the M4 at any reasonable combat range while at the same time being impervious to fire from the M4's 75mm gun except at close range, or from the rear. Fortunately, the Tiger was deployed in very small numbers and seldom encountered in combat.

Contact with the Tiger led to a reassessment of the design of the T23E3. The Armored Force changed its opinion about the design, calling for heavier armor and a larger gun. Nevertheless, the T23 remained the pet project of Ordnance and production of 250 tanks started in November 1943 and lasted through December 1944. However, in view of Armored Force opinion, in May 1943 two more T20 derivatives entered development. The T25 was fitted with 3in. (75mm) frontal armor, weighed 36 tons, and was armed with a 90mm gun. The T26 was essentially the same but with 4in. (100mm) frontal armor so it weighed 40 tons. Testing of the T23 in the summer of 1943 revealed serious shortcomings of the electric drive transmission, and although some pilots of the T25 and T26 were completed with electric

The T23 served as the test-bed for a new electric drive system which ultimately proved to be the undoing of the design. Had it been fitted with a more dependable transmission, the T23 might have entered service in 1944 as a replacement for the Sherman. This is the second pilot of the series in March 1943 and is armed with a 76mm gun. (Patton Museum)

drive, it became evident that this design was flawed, so the main effort turned towards development of the T25E1 and T26E1 with a torquematic transmission. The latter used a fluid torque converter and a planetary transmission with manual gear selection. A total of 40 T25E1 and 10 T26E1 prototypes were completed at the Grand Blanc tank arsenal from February to May 1944.

With the invasion of France planned for the summer of 1944, the US Army began final steps to prepare its forces for combat in the main European theater. Unless a new tank was authorized by the fall of 1943, there would be very little chance of any being available by the following summer. The former head of the Armored Force, LtGen Devers, was temporary commander of US forces in the ETO until Eisenhower's later appointment. Devers was well aware that US forces had encountered Tigers again, on Sicily in July 1943, and so wanted to make certain that they could better deal with this threat. He requested that development of the T26E1 be accelerated and that 250 be manufactured as quickly as possible on a scale of one per five M4 Medium tanks. Ordnance agreed, but wanted to produce 1,000 of the T23 as well. The War Department forwarded these conflicting recommendations to the AGF for review, but LtGen McNair turned down the request. His rationale helps illuminate US Army official policy of the time:

Limited production of the T23 began in November 1943, and this is the first production pilot. By this stage the design incorporated a new turret and reverted back to the vertical volute suspension already in use on the M4 Medium tank. Troop trials raised serious doubts about the tank's reliability, and the Armored Force refused to deploy any in combat. The T23 tank's turret was used to modernize the M4 tank with a 76mm gun. (Patton Museum)

"The M4 tank, particularly the M4A3, has been widely hailed as the best tank on the battlefield today. There are indications that the enemy concurs in this view. Apparently, the M4 is an ideal combination of mobility, dependability, speed, protection, and firepower. Other than this particular request – which represents the British view – there has been no call from any theater for a 90mm tank gun. There appears to be no fear on the part of our forces of the German Mark VI (Tiger) tank … There can be no basis for the T26 tank other than the conception of a tank versus tank duel – which is believed unsound and unnecessary. Both British and American battle experience has demonstrated that the antitank gun in suitable numbers and disposed properly is the master of the tank. Any attempt to armor and gun tanks so as to outmatch antitank guns is foredoomed to failure … There is no indication that the 76mm anti-tank gun is inadequate against the German Mark VI (Tiger) tank."

Aside from being technically inaccurate, McNair's argument reflects the smugness and complacency in US Army doctrine prior to the Normandy invasion. McNair was not alone in this belief: the idea that the 76mm gun was able to deal with the Tiger was widely held in the US Army in 1943, and was quite wrong. The Armored Force did not support replacing the 75mm gun with the 76mm gun, only supplementing it in a ratio of about one 76mm gun tank per three normal 75mm gun tanks. The Armored Force felt that the 76mm gun's only advantage was that it had slightly better anti-armor penetration; it fired a poorer high-explosive round. In addition, it had such severe muzzle blast that it made the accurate aiming of a second round difficult. The preference for the older 75mm gun was based on the doctrine that the tank's main role was exploitation and that anti-tank capability was secondary to the tank's mission. The 76mm gun firing the M62 APC (Armor-piercing, capped) projectile had a nominal penetration of 109mm at 500 yards with the armor angled at 20 degrees. The Tiger's gun mantlet was 120mm thick and the hull front was

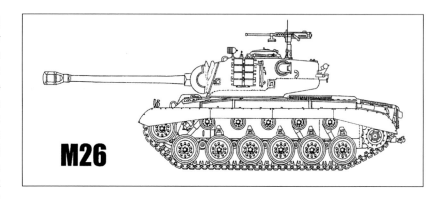

M26

100mm thick. In practice, the 76mm gun could only penetrate the Tiger mantlet at ranges of 100m or less and the hull at 400m, while the Tiger could inflict penetration of the M4 Sherman at more than double these ranges. Until the new 76mm hypervelocity armor piercing ammunition (HVAP) became available in small quantities in late 1944, the 76mm gun was usually ineffective against the Tiger in combat.

Armor penetration of US tank guns
(at 500 yards range, homogeneous armor plate at 30 degrees)

Gun	Round	Type	Penetration in mm
75mm M3	M61	APC	66
75mm M3	M72	AP	76
76mm M1	M62	APC	93
76mm M1	M79	AP	109
76mm M1	M93	HVAP	157
90mm M3	M82	APC	120
90mm M3	T33	AP	119
90mm M3	T30E16	HVAP	221
90mm T15E2	T43	AP	132
90mm T15E2	T44	HVAP	244

Encounters with the German Tiger tank in Tunisia and Sicily in 1943 convinced the Armored Force of the need for a heavy tank with better armor and firepower than the T23 Medium tank. Two designs were examined, the T25 seen here with 3in. frontal hull armor and the T26 with 4in. hull armor. The initial pilots in January 1944, like the T25 seen here, used horizontal volute spring suspension, but this was quickly superceded by torsion bar suspension. (Patton Museum)

While McNair continued to argue the effectiveness of tank destroyers, there was no battlefield experience to validate this notion. The performance of the tank destroyers in Tunisia had been unremarkable, though McNair had blamed this on a failure to adhere to proper tactics. However, the problem was the basic concept. The idea of a tank destroyer had emerged in the summer of 1940 as a defensive antidote to the style of German blitzkrieg warfare used against France that year. Under this scheme, towed or self-propelled tank destroyers would be maintained in a corps reserve, and then sent in mass to defeat any German armored breakthrough. The essentially defensive nature of this undermined its value to the US Army in 1944, since it did not fully address how tank destroyers could contribute to offensive mobile warfare. Under the battlefield conditions of 1944, German tanks rarely appeared in mass concentrations, and tank destroyers were seldom available when and where they were needed. The tank destroyer concept would be abandoned as a failure after the war.

The Army's complacency about the adequacy of the 76mm gun confused field commanders who might otherwise have supported Devers' request for the T26E1. In December 1943 Eisenhower refused to support the T26E1 request since he felt that its only advantage was the heavier armor. He did not feel that such a heavy tank was needed for the armor protection alone, and he failed to appreciate the substantial advantage that its 90mm gun offered. Eisenhower had been informed repeatedly that the 76mm gun would prove more than adequate against new German tanks, and after Normandy he would bitterly charge that he had been deceived on the tank gun issue.

Devers continued to press the case for the T26E1, and the Army Service Forces finally requested that the War Department itself attempt to settle the issue. On December 16, 1943, the War Department issued a directive that authorized the production of 250 T26E1 tanks by April 1945. The AGF continued to oppose the directive, this time on technical grounds. They argued that torsion bar suspension had never been used on a tank even half as heavy as the T26E1, that the powerplant was inadequate, and that the torquematic transmission had only been used on light vehicles such as the M18 tank destroyer. The argument ignored the fact that both the German Tiger and Soviet KV and IS heavy tanks used torsion bar suspension, and that torquematic transmission was more mature than other options such as the T23's troublesome electric drive. These arguments were ignored. To his credit, McNair backed off from further opposition to the program since a higher command authority had rejected the arguments of his office.

While Devers wanted the T26E1 tank program accelerated, there was little consensus in the combat arms. After a presentation about the new tank in England in January 1944, the future 3rd Armored Division commander, Brig(Gen) Maurice Rose, strongly supported accelerating the program because of his previous contact with the German Tiger tank in combat in Sicily. On the other hand, the future Third Army commander, Gen George S. Patton, opposed the plan. Patton was a far more influential tank commander than Rose, and his opinion held sway among senior US Army leaders in England. Patton also opposed the deployment of the new M4 Medium tanks with 76mm gun, arguing that the existing 75mm gun was more than adequate. Although Patton was unquestionably the finest practitioner of mechanized combat in the US Army in World War II, his technical judgment was frequently poor. General Bruce Clarke, who commanded US armored units during the tank battles in Lorraine in September 1944 and at St. Vith in the Ardennes in December 1944, later remarked: "Patton knew as little about tanks as anyone I know."

While the AGF no longer opposed manufacturing a new tank, it was not finished meddling with the program. Lieutenant-General McNair

The nemesis of the M4 Sherman tank in Europe in 1944–45 was the German Panther tank. While superior to the M4 in firepower, armor, and mobility, they could be overcome. These are three Panther Ausf. G tanks of the 9.Panzer-Division knocked out near Humain, Belgium, during a counter-attack against the US 2nd Armored Division on December 26/27, 1944. The shortcomings of the M4 Medium tank during the Battle of the Bulge resulted in greater pressure to field the T26 Heavy tank. (US Army)

favored the lighter T25E1 over the heavier and better armored T26E1 and he proposed switching the gun on the T25E1 from the 90mm gun back to the lighter 76mm gun and incorporating the wider tracks of the T26E1. His argument was that the resulting design would be almost as mobile as the M4 Medium tank while being adequately armed. Instead, the War Department sent his recommendation into limbo while at the same time increasing T26E1 production to 2,000 tanks, of which 200 would be armed with 105mm howitzers and the rest with 90mm guns.

These arguments had an air of academic unreality about them, since they largely omitted to address what the Germans might field in the summer 1944 battles. There had been a continual arms race in tank guns, anti-tank guns, and tank armor on the Eastern Front. In the summer of 1943 the Wehrmacht had finally introduced the new Panther medium tank into combat during the titanic tank battles at Kursk on the Eastern Front. The Panther had been developed in response to the Soviet T-34, and was arguably the finest tank of the war. US Army intelligence was aware of the technical specifications of the Panther, since the military attaché in Moscow had been allowed to inspect a captured example at an exhibit, and its details were contained in widely distributed technical intelligence reports published in the fall of 1943. Although the Panther was not as thickly armored as the Tiger in the front, its armor was better angled, giving it greater effective armor thickness in front. Its glacis plate was 80–85mm thick, giving it an equivalent thickness of 185mm. As a result, the Panther's gun mantlet was vulnerable to the US Army's 76mm gun only at ranges of 100m or less, while its hull front was essentially invulnerable at any range.

Although the technical features of the Panther were correctly noted, the US Army ignored the new tank's importance. At first the Panther was seen as a heavy tank that would be deployed in separate battalions like the Tiger, implying that it would be fielded in modest numbers. This was completely wrong. The Panther was intended as a medium tank to replace the PzKpfw IV. Unlike the Tiger, it would be manufactured in very large numbers, so that by the time of the Normandy invasion, in June 1944, almost half the German medium tank force in France were Panthers. Instead of being encountered on relatively rare occasions, which had been the US experience with the Tiger in 1943, the Panther would become a major threat to US tank units in France.

This failure to appreciate the Panther threat was a significant failure of the US Army leadership prior to the Normandy invasion. US commanders were insufficiently experienced to appreciate the dynamics of tank technology and were distracted by the fundamental flaws in their tank and tank destroyer doctrine. The British Army, which had seen the continual increase in German tank firepower since 1939, was already working on a more potent tank gun, the 17-pdr, even before the Panther appeared. Due to their combat experience, the British anticipated that the Germans would field tanks with better guns and better armor by 1944, even though they had no specific information when the 17-pdr gun program was begun. By the time of the Normandy invasion, the British were able to field one Sherman tank armed with the 17-pdr in each tank troop. While not a perfect solution, it did mean that the British tank units could deal with Panther and Tiger tanks with a greater chance of success.

It is extremely unlikely that the T26E1 tank could have been fielded in Normandy in 1944, and not merely because of the resistance of the

Another view of a T26E3 of Grimball's platoon on the road between Thum and Ginnick, Germany, on March 1, 1945, shortly before the Remagen operation. In the background is a T5E1 armored recovery vehicle pushing a set of T1E1 mine exploders. (US Army)

AGF. Its design had not progressed far enough in the fall of 1943 for there to have been much chance of deploying it so quickly. By way of comparison, work on the M4A3E2 Assault, a more heavily armored version of the M4A3 Medium tank, was begun in February 1944 and the first tanks were fielded about eight months later, in the early fall of 1944. However, the M4A3E2 was only a modification of the M4 tank, not a wholly new design like the T26E1. A more appropriate comparison would be another new design, like the German Panther, British Centurion, or Soviet IS-2. Design of the German Panther began in the summer of 1941 and it was not fielded until two years later, in summer 1943. The British Centurion design, which began in late 1943, after the T26E1, was first trialed shortly after the end of the war in Europe, in May 1945. The Red Army, after the shock of the Tiger and Panther at Kursk, accelerated the IS-2 development and fielded it in about seven months from the summer of 1943 to February 1944. The Pershing's development was not unduly protracted when compared to the Panther or Centurion, but neither did it show the urgency of the Soviet IS-2's rapid introduction into service.

Had the US Army better appreciated the threat posed by the Panther, a more likely course would have been to modify the M4 with a more potent gun, much as the Soviets did with the T-34-85. Acceleration of the fielding of 76mm HVAP ammunition would have been one short-term solution, and a 90mm gun on the M4 was not out of the question. Had their been more enthusiasm for a better tank like the T26E1 in the fall of 1943, the first units might have deployed during the Battle of the Bulge in December 1944 rather than during the campaign in Germany three months later. For the M26 to have reached combat in June 1944, its production would have had to begin by the fall of 1943, when in fact the first prototypes were not completed until February 1944.

The 3rd Armored Division was the recipient of the most powerful US tank deployed in World War II, a pilot for the T26E4 armed with the T15 90mm gun. By this stage the division's ordnance team had already installed applique armor on the glacis plate and gun mantlet, though additional armor was later added to cover the turret front. This tank fired its gun in anger only once during the fighting, on April 4, 1945, against an unidentified heavy armored vehicle. (Patton Museum)

The Normandy Tank Crisis

The US Army committed two armored divisions and seven separate tank battalions to the initial fighting in Normandy in June 1944. After having been repeatedly told that the M4 was "the best tank on the battlefield," they were shocked by the heavy losses suffered in the initial fighting. The M4 proved vulnerable to virtually all German anti-tank weapons, including the towed 75mm Pak 40 anti-tank and the man-portable Panzerschreck rocket launcher. In the first month of fighting, M4 Medium tank casualties were 32 per cent of the available strength, more than four times its expected attrition rate of 7 per cent. Although the M4 could fight on near equal terms with the PzKpfw IV tank, it was unable to penetrate the frontal armor of the new Panther tank, either with the

75mm gun or the new 76mm gun. The hedgerow country of Normandy made it very difficult to outmaneuver the German tanks to attack their weaker side armor, and therefore tank-vs-tank encounters with the Panther proved to be very one-sided.

The Normandy fighting ended once and for all the debate about whether tank destroyers could single-handedly deal with the armor threat. They could not. Tanks, whether in separate tank battalions or in the armored divisions, regularly encountered German tanks and had to be able to deal with them on a near-equal basis. The tank destroyer concept might have worked had the US Army been on the defensive, like the French Army in 1940, but due to the offensive nature of American operations in 1944, it was a failure, and it undermined the capabilities of the US Army.

There was a firestorm of criticism of US tank designs. As the 12th Army Group's Armor Section later reported: "Our experience in the early hedgerow fighting indicated that our main tank armament was no match for the front armor of the German Panther and Tiger tanks and we realized that more open operations would make this condition still more unpleasant." The bulk of the German panzer divisions in Normandy were opposite the British Army, but this might change once the US Army led the break-out. On July 12, 1944, a special board of officers from the First Army was formed to determine which US weapons might be capable of defeating the Panther and Tiger. Captured examples of the two tanks were placed in a field and then fired on using different types of guns and ammunition. None of the available US weapons could penetrate the Panther frontally, though some could do so against the side and rear, depending on range. When told of the problem, Eisenhower remarked bitterly: "You mean our 76 won't knock these Panthers out? Why, I thought it was going to be the wonder gun of the war… Why is it that I'm the last to hear about this stuff? Ordnance told me this 76 would take care of anything the Germans had. Now I find you can't knock out a damn thing with it."

As a short term solution, the program to field a new tank destroyer was accelerated. The M36 gun motor carriage, armed with the same 90mm gun as the T26, was fielded in the fall of 1944. Although the new gun was much appreciated, tankers had given up on the tank destroyer idea and wanted "a killer tank, not a tank killer."

Heavy tank losses to Japanese 47mm anti-tank guns on Okinawa led to the dispatch of a trials batch of M26 tanks to the Pacific. The M26 Pershing tanks did not arrive on Okinawa until July 21,1945, after the fighting had ended. They were to be used in the anticipated invasion of the Japanese Home Islands, but the war was over before they saw combat. (US Army)

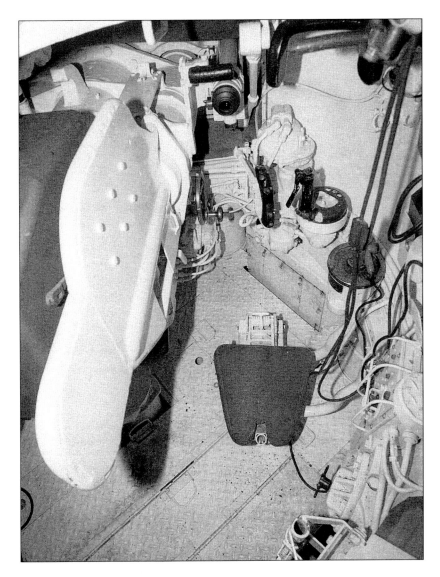

A view inside the turret of the M26, looking from the commander's station in the right side down towards the gunner's station. The gun breech is to the left, and the gunner's fire controls are evident towards the top of the photo. This is from inside a preserved M26 at the Patton Museum at Ft. Knox. (Author)

The AGF was still pushing for Ordnance to develop a version of the T25E1 and T26E1 with 75mm and 76mm guns as late as August 1944, even after the tank controversy in Normandy. However, once the storm of complaints began to arrive from Europe, these suggestions retreated into well deserved obscurity. Instead, there was pressure to deploy a trials platoon of T26E1 tanks in Europe as quickly as possible, a plan which the AGF strongly resisted. Ordnance tried to accelerate the standardization of the T26E1 before engineering trials were complete, a process that the AGF also opposed. To further confuse matters, Ordnance was still pushing for possible deployment of the troubled T23 tank with the 76mm gun. User trials of the T23 by the 758th Tank Battalion in the spring of 1944 had convinced the Armored Force that it was a fundamentally flawed design and that the electric drive transmission was not battle-worthy. However, having pushed for the construction of 250 of these tanks, Ordnance would not let the matter rest, and continued to argue for combat trials even in 1945. None was sent overseas, nor was the design ever standardized due to its lingering problems, and Ordnance's advocacy of the flawed T23 only served to undermine confidence in its judgment about the T26E1.

THE PERSHING TANK EMERGES

Before the controversy over the future of US tank design, the T25E1 and T26E1 had entered trials, in the late spring of 1944. Compared to the troubled T23, the T26E1 trials went relatively smoothly. They were successful enough that on June 15, 1944, the War Department decided that the 1945 tank production program would be changed to permit production of 6,000 T26 tanks. Trials of the T26E1 did not conclude until the end of 1944, and the testing program uncovered a substantial number of significant modifications that would be needed before series production could start. As a result, the series production version with the 90mm gun was designated as the T26E3 Heavy tank and the assault gun version with the 105mm howitzer was designated as T26E2.

Series production of the T26E3 began in November 1944 at the Grand Blanc tank arsenal and followed in March 1945 at the Detroit tank arsenal. By the time the war ended in Europe a total of 705 T26E3 tanks had been manufactured. After standardization, it became the M26 tank, though it was often called the M26E3 by troops in the ETO in 1945. It had not been the practice of the US Army to name its tanks during World War II. After the war, many US tanks became better known by the names the British gave them – such as Stuart, Grant, and Sherman. As a result, the US Army began an unofficial policy of naming its new tanks, and the M26 was named the Pershing, after the commander of US troops in World War I, John "Black Jack" Pershing.

A view of the loader's station in the M26 Pershing. The assemblies in the lower left of the photo are the ready racks, each of which holds two rounds of 90mm ammunition. In the center right is the mount for the co-axial .30 cal machine gun. (Author)

Pressure to field a new tank abated in the fall of 1944. The rate of tank loss decreased to more moderate levels after the breakout from Normandy in August 1944 and the following month tank units of Patton's Third Army shattered a local panzer counteroffensive in Lorraine. Even though Patton's units were equipped almost entirely with the 75mm gun versions of the M4 Medium tank, the US units inflicted disproportionate losses on German Panther units due to better training and tactics. The head of the 12th Army Group's armored vehicle section wrote back to Washington: "Probably the problem of the Panther will no longer be with us for the remainder of the war. The German, we believe, has lost most of his armor."

The most pressing issue for US tank commanders in the fall of 1944 was the need to increase tank replacements amidst lingering after-effects

Development of the M26 continued after the war. The T26E4 was fitted with the T15 gun. Although powerful, its two-piece ammunition made the Army reluctant to accept it for service. This tank has been fitted with an experimental twin .50 cal machine gun mounting over the loader's station. (Patton Museum)

of the Normandy losses and insufficient tank reserves in the theater. Tank units were regularly operating at below unit strength, and replacements were not arriving fast enough. The situation worsened abruptly in December 1944 after the Germans launched the Battle of the Bulge in the Ardennes. US tank losses again began to climb to alarming levels, exacerbated by the shortage of replacements. The German units were equipped not only with the Panther tank, but with the new King Tiger tank and improved tank destroyers. Complaints about the poor quality of American tanks reached the press and became a public scandal in the United States.

By the end of 1944, a total of 40 T26E3 tanks had been completed. There was pressure to do something in response to the criticism coming from Europe. The head of Ordnance research, MajGen G.M. Barnes, suggested sending half the new tanks to Europe for impromptu combat trials while the other 20 went to Ft. Knox for the usual tests. AGF objected to the plan but finally relented when Barnes threatened to bring the issue before the Army Chief of Staff himself, Gen George C. Marshall. The first batch of 20 T26E3s was shipped to Antwerp and arrived in January 1945. This was part of a larger effort called the Zebra Mission, which included dispatch of other new weapons to deal with the German tank threat, such as new anti-tank guns.

To gather first-hand evidence of the technical problems of US armor, the Zebra Mission team included senior army officials involved in tank policy. All 20 T26E3 tanks were assigned to Gen Bradley's 12th Army Group and were sent to First Army. They were split into two groups, with ten each going to the 3rd and 9th Armored Divisions. The Zebra Mission's T26E3 team was led by Capt Elmer Gray, accompanied by a civilian expert on the 90mm gun from Aberdeen Proving Ground, Slim Price. Training for the 3rd Armored Division crews concluded on 20 February; the 9th Armored Division crews finished at the end of the month.

The T26E3 tanks were scattered in various companies of the 3rd Armored Division and committed to combat on February 25, 1945, with Task Force Lovelady during the fighting for the Roer River. The first tank was lost on 26 February when it was ambushed at night near Elsdorf by a Tiger I tank, probably from Pz.Abt.301. Two crewmen were killed, but the tank was repaired and put back into action a few days later. The next day, a T26E3 of Co.E, 33rd Armored Regiment knocked out a Tiger I and two PzKpfw IV tanks from the 9.Pz.Div. near Elsdorf. The Tiger was hit at a range of about 900 yards with a round of the new T30E16 HVAP,

Development of a more powerful 90mm gun continued with the M26E1, which used the improved T54 90mm gun with single-piece fixed ammunition. It did not enter production due to low Army budgets in the late 1940s. (Patton Museum)

followed by a round of normal T33 armor piercing, which entered the turret and set off an internal explosion. The two PzKpfw IVs were knocked out at the impressive range of 1,200 yards, beyond the normal engagement ranges for US tanks in World War II.

The T26E3 tanks with the 9th Armored Division were committed to action during the Roer fighting in late February 1945. One tank was disabled on the night of March 1, 1945, when hit twice by a 150mm field gun. This left the T26E3 tank platoon of the 14th Tank Battalion down to four tanks when it took part in one of the most famous actions of World War II. On March 7, 1945 infantry half-tracks of Combat Command B, 9th Armored Division crested a hill overlooking the town of Remagen on the Rhine River. Amazingly, the massive Ludendorf railroad bridge was still standing, even though nearly every other bridge over the Rhine had been destroyed by the Germans to prevent the Allies crossing. The local German commander had hesitated to drop the bridge, trying the extract a large number of his troops still on the western bank of the Rhine. Armored infantry supported by Lt John Grimball's T26E3 platoon fought their way through the town and reached the approaches to the bridge around 1400hrs. The Germans detonated a large explosive charge on the approach causeway, preventing the tanks from crossing. As the US infantry and engineers prepared to cross on foot, the Germans detonated their main explosive devices on the bridge. The explosion damaged the bridge, but the charge was not sufficient to drop any of the spans, since only second grade commercial explosive had been used. The T26E3 tanks provided covering fire as the infantry moved across, with Grimball's tank knocking out a machine gun nest in one of the towers on the opposite bank. A German troop train was spotted moving on the east bank of the river, unaware of the fighting, and the locomotive was destroyed by 90mm high explosive fire from the tanks.

The only Zebra Mission T26E3 tank totally destroyed during the war was lost during the fighting near Cologne in early March. It was hit at point blank range by an 88mm shell from a Nashorn self-propelled gun

Encounters with the German Tiger I led to the development of an even heavier tank than the Pershing. This is the T34 prototype in 1945, armed with a 120mm gun derived from the 120mm anti-aircraft gun. Although influenced by the Pershing design, the T29, T30, and T34 Heavy tanks all differed substantially in powerplant, turret, and features. None entered series production due to the end of the war. (MHI)

which set off the turret ammunition. Later fighting, on March 6, 1945, led to one of the most famous tank-vs-tank engagements of the war. A Panther tank from 9.Pz.Div. stationed in the courtyard in front of the cathedral in Cologne ambushed an M4 Medium tank as it approached. The T26E3 tank of Sgt Bob Early from Co.E, 32nd Armored Regiment, 3rd Armored Division was sent to deal with it and charged the Panther from the side. The Panther was still slowly turning its turret towards its opponents when the first of three rounds slammed into it, causing an internal fire that destroyed the tank. The duel was captured on film by a signal corps cameraman and the footage frequently appears in documentaries about the war, seldom with correct identification. The same day, other T26E3 tanks from the 3rd Armored Division knocked out a Tiger I and a PzKpfw IV near the city.

In mid-March an additional T26 arrived in Germany, fresh from gunnery trials in the United States. This was the sole example of the so-called "Super Pershing" to see combat – an original T26E1 pilot tank which had been re-armed with a new long-barreled T15E1 90mm gun that was designed to offer performance comparable to the German 88mm KwK 43 on the King Tiger. The T15E1 gun could penetrate 220mm of armor at 1,000 yards at 30 degrees using the new T30E16 tungsten carbide HVAP round. On arrival at the 3rd Armored Division, the ordnance battalion decided to enhance the Super Pershing with additional armor plate to

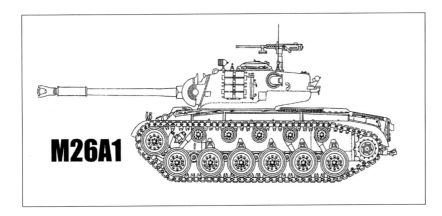

M26A1

bring it closer to the armor on the King Tiger. The 5 tons of applique armor were designed and fabricated using layers of 40mm boiler plate on the hull and a plate of 80mm armor taken from a German Panther on the gun mantlet. This tank got to fire its gun in anger on only one occasion on April 4, 1945 – when it engaged and destroyed a German armored vehicle, probably a Tiger or Panther, at a range of 1,500 yards, during the fighting along the Weser River.

A second batch of T26E3 tanks arrived in Antwerp late in March. They were delivered to the Ninth Army and were divided between the 2nd Armored Division (22 tanks) and the 5th Armored Division (18 tanks). A subsequent batch of 30 tanks was allotted to Patton's Third Army in April, all going to the 11th Armored Division. This was the last unit equipped with the T26E3 to use it in combat. In the final weeks of the war, the T26E3 tanks saw less combat due to the collapse of the German armed forces.

By the end of the war, 310 T26E3 tanks had been delivered to Europe, of which 200 had been issued to tank units. However, it was only the tanks supplied in February 1945 that saw extensive combat. The Pershing experience can best be summed up as "too little, too late." A post-war report by First Army assessed the combat trials of the Zebra Mission: "Unfortunately for this test, the German armor had been so crippled as to present a very poor opponent and the cessation of hostilities so soon after forming these companies precluded the gaining of any real experience."

The T26E3 tank was received with enthusiasm by US tankers, since it offered substantially better armor and firepower than the M4 Medium tank. However, it had been rushed into service and so had a predictable number of mechanical problems. An Ordnance report prepared after the war included a four-page list of all of the minor automotive problems that cropped up with the T26E3. The two most serious tactical complaints were its lack of range and its sluggish automotive per-formance. It was powered by the same engine as the M4A3 Medium tank, which weighed about ten tons less, and so it was significantly slower. Other problems included the small size of the hatches, especially in the hull front. Many small improvements were incorporated into pro-duction, which continued until October 1945. The final drive assembly had

The T84 8in. howitzer motor carriage was one of a number of self-propelled artillery vehicles developed on the basis of M26 Pershing components. The hull configuration was reversed, with the engine and transmission now located in front. This weapon was not accepted for series production due to the end of the war. (Patton Museum)

An even heavier weapon than the T84 was the T92 240mm howitzer motor carriage. The sheer size of the howitzer required the addition of another road-wheel station and other substantial changes to the design. Five of these were built in 1945, but no production ensued due to the end of the war. (Patton Museum)

external reinforcements added to correct the problem of the assembly shaking loose. Turnbuckles were added to the front and rear of the fenders to prevent them from drooping into the upper run of track when weighted down with stowage. There were also quite a number of small automotive changes, and many were retrofitted onto vehicles already in the field.

The T26E3 had one more combat mission in World War II. During the fighting on Okinawa in April and May 1945 combat losses on the M4 Medium tanks proved higher than expected due to the prevalence of Japanese 47mm anti-tank guns. Ordnance decided to ship a small number of T26E3 tanks now designated M26 after having been type classified for combat trials. The dozen M26 tanks did not arrive on Okinawa until July 21, 1945, after the fighting had ended. As preparations were underway for the invasion of Japan, the tanks were divided between the 193rd and 711th Tank Battalions for training, in anticipation of later combat use on the Japanese Home Islands. This, of course, never transpired, so the M26 did not see combat in the Pacific theater during World War II.

LATE-WAR DEVELOPMENTS

From 1944 there were plans to produce the T26E2 howitzer tank version of the T26, armed with a 105mm howitzer. This was intended to be used in the headquarter companies of the T26E3 battalions, much as the M4 105mm howitzer tanks had been used. Such vehicles provided indirect fire-support for the tank battalions. There had also been some consideration given to fielding the howitzer tank for use as an assault tank like the M4A3E2 Jumbo. This program did not have high priority, and the pilot was only delivered for trials in July 1945. After service acceptance, the howitzer tank was designated as M45. Due to the lighter weight of the M4 105mm howitzer, the M45 had a thicker gun mantlet than the normal T26E3 tank, fully 8ins. (200mm), to balance the weight of the turret. With the war in Europe ending, production requirements dropped precipitously, and only 185 M45 105mm tanks were completed, starting in July 1945. A small number were used in combat in Korea in 1950–53.

The final version of the M26 produced during the war was the T26E5. This was an attempt at producing an assault tank comparable to the M4A3E2 "Jumbo" of the Sherman family. It had increased thickness of the hull front (to 152mm) and the turret front (to 190mm). A total of 27 of these were built from June 1945, and they were only used for test purposes after the war. The project was revived after the war in modified form as the T32 Heavy tank, but only two pilots were built.

Work also continued on versions of the T26 armed with a more powerful gun. The T26E1 Super Pershing fitted with the experimental T15 90mm gun was an expedient, and work shifted to the T26E4, using the gun in an improved mount which did not require the improvised exterior springs. A total of 25 of these vehicles were completed in 1945. The main problem with this tank was that the gun used a split ammunition, with separate projectile and propellant casing, which reduced the rate of fire of the weapon. Although there had been plans to build 1,000 of these in place of the normal M26, with the end of the war work shifted to the T54 gun, which had the ballistic characteristics of the earlier weapon but introduced a one-piece round that would be easier to handle inside the turret. Further work on this design was undertaken after the war on the M26E1. This introduced improvements inside the turret, such as a concentric recoil mechanism intended to take up less internal space. Firing trials of the M26E1 were conducted at Aberdeen Proving Ground from February 1947 to January 1949. These indicated that the gun offered superior performance to any other tank gun then in service. However, given the restricted budgets of the immediate post-war years and the lack of any pressing requirement for such a weapon, the program slipped into limbo. Another weapon tested on the M26E1 was the 3-inch T98, a hypervelocity cannon based on the Navy's 3in. gun.

Through most of 1944 there was little demand in the Armored Force for a heavy tank to challenge the Tiger, but Ordnance considered using the T26 as the basis for such a vehicle, armed with extremely powerful guns. This development of the T29 and T30 Heavy tanks began in September 1944. Although the parentage of the T29 and T30 was clear from the hull front and suspension, in fact the designs were significantly different from the T26 tank. The chassis was lengthened to accommodate the extra weight of the larger turret, a more powerful

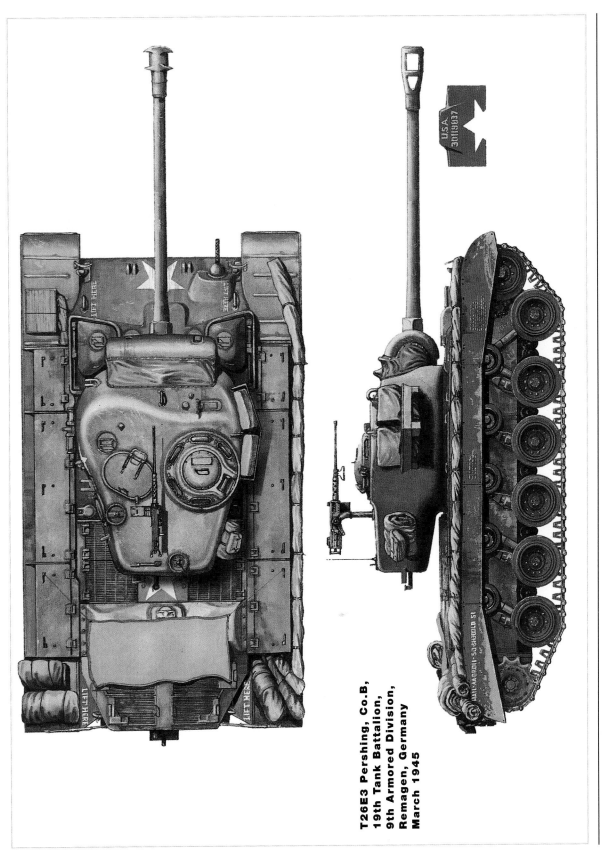

**T26E3 Pershing, Co.B,
19th Tank Battalion,
9th Armored Division,
Remagen, Germany
March 1945**

A

B

**T26E1 Super Pershing,
33rd Armored Regiment,
3rd Armored Division,
Germany,
March 1945**

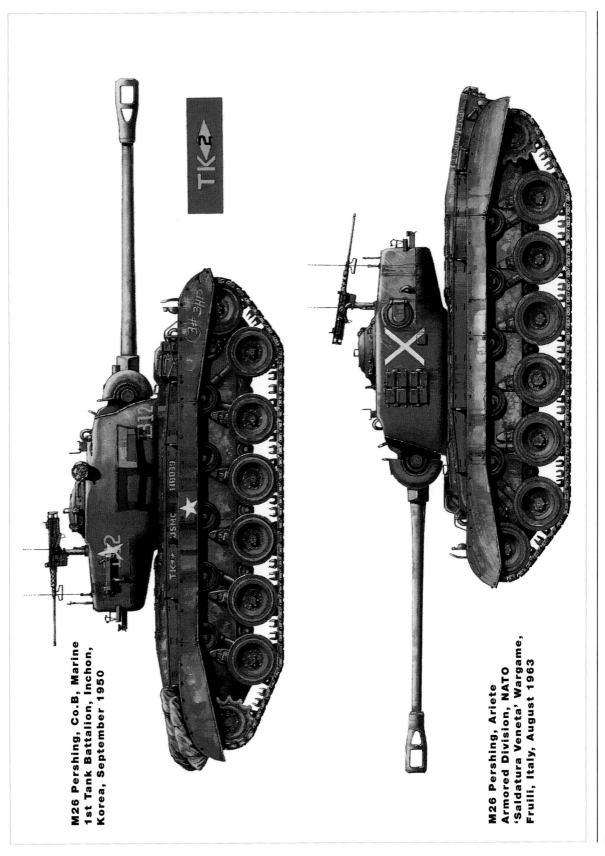

M26 Pershing, Co.B, Marine 1st Tank Battalion, Inchon, Korea, September 1950

M26 Pershing, Ariete Armored Division, NATO 'Saldatura Veneta' Wargame, Fruili, Italy, August 1963

M26 PERSHING TANK, US ARMY 1945

KEY

1 Muzzle brake
2 .30 cal co-axial machine gun
3 Gunner's seat
4 90mm gun breech
5 Loader's hatch
6 radio antenna
7 Commander's hatch
8 Browning M2 .50 cal. machine gun
9 Commander's seat (folded up)
10 Stowage rack for front hatch weather covers
11 Hull ammunition stowage
12 Tank radio
13 Stowage mounts for .50 cal. machine gun
14 Engine
15 Transmission
16 Engine radiators
17 Exhaust pipes
18 Transmission access armored grills
19 gun travel lock
20 drive sprocket
21 track end connector
22 First aid container
23 Stowage pannier
24 side skirt
25 return roller
26 roadwheel
27 adjustable idler wheel
28 fender support tunbuckle
29 Headlight
30 Driver's hatch and periscope
31 Drier's controls
32 Driver's instrument panel
33 Hull front ventilator

SPECIFICATION

Crew: 5 (commander, gunner, loader, driver, co-driver)

Combat weight: 46.1 tons

Power-to-weight ratio: 10.8 hp/t

Overall length: 340ins.

Width: 138ins.

Height: 109ins.

Engine: Ford GAF 8 cylinder liquid cooled, 4 cycle gasoline engine

Transmission: Torquematic with 3 forward, 1 reverse gear

Fuel capacity: 183 gallons

Maximum speed (road): 30mph

Maximum speed (cross-country): 20 mph

Maximum range: 100 miles

Fuel consumption: 1.8 gal/mile

Ground clearance: 17.2ins.

Armament: M3 90mm gun in M67 mount

Main gun ammunition: 70 rounds (M82 APC, T30E16 HVAP, T33 APBC-T, M71 HE)

Muzzle velocity: 2,650 fps (M82)

Penetration: 120mm @30 degrees @ 500 yards (M82 APC); 221mm @30 degrees @500 yards (T30E16 HVAP)

Maximum effective range: 21,400 yards

Gun depression/elevation: -10 to + 20 degrees

Armor: 115mm gun mantlet; 76mm turret sides; 100mm hull upper front/76mm hull lower front; 50–75mm hull sides.

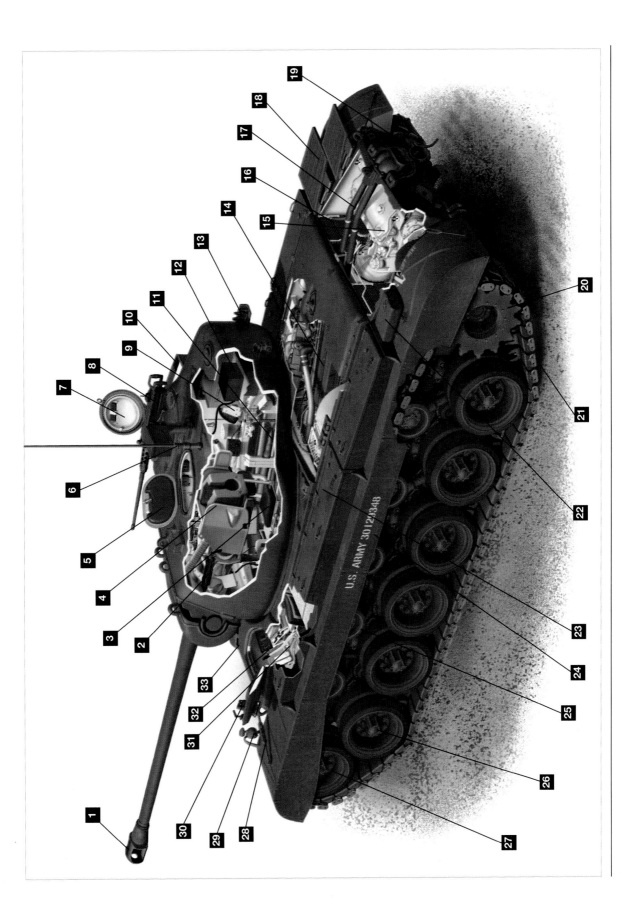

E

**M46 Patton, Co.C, 6th Tank Battalion,
Han River, February 1951**

**M46 Patton, Co.A,
73rd Tank Battalion,
Han River, February 1951**

**M46 Patton,
64th Tank Battalion,
Han River, February 1951**

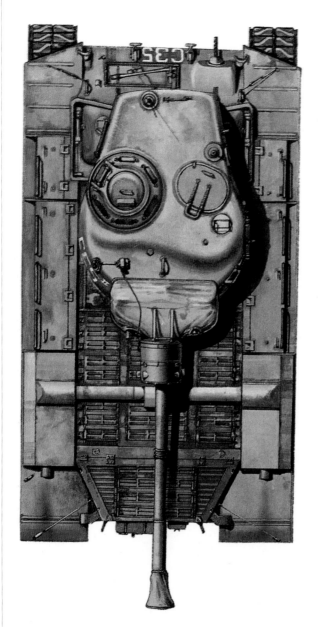

**M46 Patton, Co.C,
Marine 1st Tank Battalion,
Korea, 1952**

The M46 was developed as a rebuild program for the M26 shortly before the outbreak of the Korean War. A new powerpack was installed in the rear hull, leading to modified engine access doors and a different rear panel. Like the M26A1, it was armed with the M3A1 90mm gun, which had a fume extractor and a new muzzle brake. The M46 is most easily distinguished from the M26A1 by the large mufflers on the fender and the addition of a track tension idler wheel below the drive sprocket. Here, an M46 Patton of Co.C, 6th Tank Battalion fires its 90mm gun while supporting the 24th Infantry Division near Song Sil-li, Korea, on January 10, 1952. (US Army)

engine was introduced, and the turrets were completely different. The T29 mounted a T5E1 105mm long-barreled gun, and the T30 was armed with a T7 155mm gun.

A third prototype was introduced in April 1945, the T34, armed with a 120mm gun. After contact with the German King Tiger heavy tank in the Ardennes in December 1944, interest from the Armored Force in fielding these heavy tanks increased considerably. Procurement of 1,152 T29 Heavy tanks was approved on April 12, 1945. However, the war in the Pacific put an end to any production, though the prototypes remained in trials in the late 1940s and served as the basis for tests of new tank technologies such as optical range-finders.

Interest in heavy-gun tanks revived in the late 1940s due to Cold War tensions. The Soviet IS-3 Stalin heavy tank was regarded as a major threat, and so to combat it work began on the T43 tank armed with a 120mm gun. Although this was based on some of the lessons of the T29/T30/T34 effort, the T43 was a wholly new design, which had more in common with later members of the Patton tank family than with the Pershing. It later reached production and was designated as the M103 tank.

In light of experience in World War II, the US Army favored the use of a common chassis for specialized armored vehicles such as

LEFT **There were few specialized variants of the M46 Patton, since it was in essence a rebuilt M26 Pershing. One of the ten T40 pilots was rebuilt as the T39 Engineer Armored vehicle in 1951. This was fitted with a British Mark 1 6.5in. demolition gun which fired a 30-pound high-explosive-plastic (HEP) round to destroy bunkers. On the rear deck is a 20-ton winch with an associating lifting boom. It was not accepted for production, since by this time plans were underway for series production of the M47 tank. (Patton Museum)**

self-propelled artillery. Although a number of test vehicles derived from the M26 family were built in 1945, none reached the production stage. The first of these was the T84 8in. howitzer motor carriage, which used the T26 suspension and engine but had the powertrain moved to the front of the tank chassis to permit the howitzer to be fitted in the rear. An ammunition supply version was also developed, the cargo carrier T31. Beyond the pilot models, none was manufactured.

An even more powerful weapon was also considered, the T92 240mm howitzer motor carriage. Due to the enormous size of this weapon, the T26 chassis had to be stretched to accommodate it. Five T92 pilots were built, along with two similar T93 HMC, armed with an 8in. gun instead of the 240mm howitzer, but trials in the summer of 1945 showed that the chassis was not adequate for such large weapons, and no production was authorized.

To support T26 tank battalions, the T12 armored recovery vehicle was built in prototype. This was intended as a counterpart to wartime armored recovery vehicles such as the M31 on the M3 Medium tank chassis and the M32 on the M4 Medium tank. However, the T12 was not accepted for production and M26 units used armored recovery vehicles based on the M4 tank instead.

BELOW **Two Pershings take up defensive positions shortly after the first encounter between North Korean T-34-85s and M26 tanks of the 1st Marine Tank Battalion on August 17, 1950, near Waegwan in the Naktong Bulge of the Pusan perimeter. Several tanks of the North Korean 2/107th Tank Regiment began an attack on defensive positions of the 1st Marine Provisional Brigade but were destroyed by tank and bazooka fire in a short engagement. In the background is the T-34-85 tank of the battalion commander of the 2/107th Tank Regiment, tank #314, destroyed during the fighting. The turret roof, which was blown off by an internal ammunition fire, can be seen to the left of the Marine truck, about a 100 feet away from the tank. (US National Archives)**

Wartime plans had called for 6,000 M26 tanks to be built, but in the end, production halted in October 1945 at 2,212. The price of a T26E3 was $83,273, compared to $69,288 for an M4A1 (76mm). The M26 had been classified as a heavy tank, but in May 1946 it was reclassified as a medium tank due to the changing conception of US Army tank needs and programs to develop far heavier tanks in the future.

THE M46 PATTON

One of the few post-war programs involving the M26 to bear fruit was the M26E2. This began in January 1948 and took advantage of separate efforts to develop better tank engines and transmissions. The T26E2 introduced the Continental AV-1790-3 engine to the design, boosting horsepower from 500hp to 810hp. In addition, the power-pack introduced a new Allison CD-850-1 cross-drive transmission. Both new elements took up no more space or weight than earlier components yet offered a substantial increase in power. They would form the basis of the power-train in all US tanks through the M60A3 in the 1980s. The first modified M26 in the M26E2 configuration was delivered for trials to Aberdeen Proving Ground in May 1948. The trials revealed the usual number of technical problems. Although there were plans to incorporate the more powerful T54 long 90mm gun in the design, in the Army there was some resistance to introducing new and heavier ammunition when there was no perceived threat to warrant such a weapon. Instead, the M3 90mm gun was improved as the M3A1 by the use of a new bore evacuator to reduce fumes in the turret caused by firing the gun. It was also fitted with a new muzzle brake. These changes and the other automotive improvements led Ordnance to re-designate the new prototype as the T40.

The T40 program was accelerated by the Cold War as relations between the United States and the Soviet Union continued to deteriorate. A total of ten T40 pilot tanks were funded in 1948, and engineering tests began in August 1949. Although the Army wanted a wholly new tank design, they realized that this would take time. Instead, the T40 was accepted as the basis for an interim tank that could be fielded by remanufacturing the existing M26.

The modernized M26E2 was different enough from the M26 to be redesignated as the M46, and it was later renamed the "General Patton" in honor of Gen George S. Patton, Jr. Trials of the M46 went smoothly and initial funding was

An M26 Pershing of 1st Platoon, Co.B, Marine 1st Tank Battalion leads an attack by a squad from 5th Marines on 19 September, during the attack from Kimpo airbase to the Han River. This unit had converted from M4A3 (105mm) howitzer tanks shortly before deployment. (US National Archives)

provided in the 1949 budget. This covered 800 tanks, leaving 1,215 additional tanks in inventory suitable for upgrade. The first production M46 tanks arrived at Aberdeen Proving Ground in November 1949 for trials. By the time of the outbreak of the Korean War, 319 M46 Patton tanks had been completed. Ultimately, the Korean War interfered with plans to rebuild the additional M26s since tanks were needed so desperately. However, a more modest improvement program was already underway which substituted the M3A1 gun of the M46 for the older M3 gun. M26 tanks rebuilt with this features were redesignated as M26A1.

During the course of remanufacture of the M46, Ordnance completed work on what was termed the "New Production Medium Gun Tank," which would later emerge as the M47 Medium tank. This introduced a turret of better ballistic shape and new gun fire controls. It also introduced a number of changes to the power-train of the tank, though the hull was otherwise essentially the same as the M46. Since the M47 turret was not yet ready for production due to the complexity of its new fire controls, it was decided to incorporate these automotive improvements into the M46. This included the AV-1790-5B engine, the CD-850-4 transmission, a new oil cooling system, simplified electrical harness and other electronics, new brake controls, and other minor upgrades. The resulting tank was designated as the M46A1, and construction of 360 of these was authorized in February 1951. Externally they were identical to the M46, and they can only be distinguished by their registration numbers, which were 30163849 and higher.

As was the case with the Sherman, a howitzer tank version of the M26 was manufactured as the M45, which served in battalion headquarters companies to provide fire-support. The M45 was first used in combat in Korea in 1950. This M45 of the US Army's 6th Tank Battalion wades across the Naktong River during the fighting on September 18, 1950. The tanks are following a ford marked in the river by an engineer battalion that had surveyed the site earlier, as can be seen by the marker tapes to the left of the tank. (US Army)

THE PERSHING IN KOREA

The most extensive combat use of the M26 and M46 came during the Korean War in 1950–53. The invasion of South Korea by the North Korean People's Army (NKPA) in the summer of 1950 was spearheaded by T-34-85 tanks of the 105th Tank Brigade. The Republic of Korea (ROK) army was poorly equipped with anti-tank weapons, and the North Korean tanks were able to terrorize the ROK infantry with impunity. The US Army rushed forces to Korea by air, but this was mostly light infantry. Tanks were scarce in the Pacific region as US occupation forces in Japan

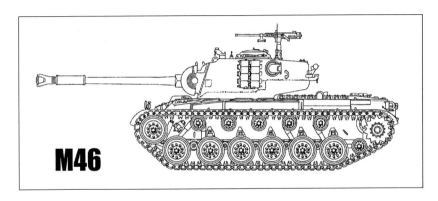

M46

had little need for them. Furthermore, they were not suitable for use in Japan because of Japan's fragile road network. Initial US attempts to stem the NKPA advance proved fruitless without tank support, so a crash effort was made to rush tank units in.

The first M26 tanks to arrive were three that had been discovered at the Tokyo Ordnance Depot. They were immobile through mechanical problems and neglect but were quickly repaired. On arrival in Korea, they were used to form a provisional tank platoon alongside a few M24 Chaffee Light tanks. The platoon was used to defend Chinju from an attack by the NKPA 6th Infantry Division on 28 July, but the M26 Pershings were in such poor mechanical state that they broke down almost immediately and were abandoned.

Aside from armored units committed to Europe, there were very few US tank units fit for rapid deployment to Korea. Four battalions were rushed into action. The 6th Tank Battalion was equipped with the new M46 Patton tank. The 70th Tank Battalion was the tank training battalion at Ft. Knox, equipped with a mixture of M4A3E8 and M26 tanks. It obtained its M26 tanks by removing the monument tanks from pedestals around the base and running them through the base depot. The 73rd Tank Battalion was the training unit from the infantry school at Ft. Benning and was equipped with M26 Pershing tanks. The 89th Tank Battalion, raised from scattered tank units in the Pacific, had a single company of M26 tanks. Besides the Army tank units, the Marine Corps activated a company from the 1st Marine Brigade and replaced their M4A3 (105mm) howitzer tanks with M26 Pershing tanks. By the time these units arrived in Korea, in August 1950, the UN forces had been pushed back into a small pocket around the port of Pusan on the southern end of the Korean peninsula opposite Japan.

The first contact between the Pershings and the NKPA tanks involved the US Marine tank company. On August 17, 1950, the 107th Tank Regiment of the NKPA 105th Armored Brigade began an attack on the 1st Marine Provisional Brigade in the Naktong Bulge of the Pusan perimeter. The lead T-34-85 encountered Marine outposts which took it under fire with bazookas which proved ineffective.

World War II experience in amphibious operations led to the development of a set of wading trunks for the M26, to permit their deployment from amphibious landing ships. On October 27, 1950, another amphibious landing was conducted at Wonson, on the eastern coast of Korea, by the 1st Marine Division as a follow-up to the Inchon landing. The M26 tanks of Co.D, Marine 1st Tank Battalion were fitted with the full deep-wading trunks for the operation to allow the tanks to be landed in the shallow harbor from LSUs. One of the tanks sits near the airbase with its wading trunks still attached. (US National Archives)

The lead tank came around a hill and encountered a Marine M26 Pershing in hull down position with only its turret exposed. Until then, the NKPA tanks had completely dominated the American M24 Light tanks, so the T-34-85 continued to charge forward, expecting another easy victory. The Marine M26 fired two 90mm armor piercing rounds into the lead tank which led to a catastrophic ammunition fire, destroying the tank. The second T-34-85 was taken under fire by the Marines with recoilless

rifles and bazookas, but was not damaged. Two M26 Pershings fired several rounds into it, leading to another ammunition fire which blew it apart. A third T-34-85 met a similar fate, so the fourth and final T-34 retreated. The T-34-85, which had caused panic in the ranks of ROK and US infantry for nearly two months, was now derisively referred to as the "Caviar Can."

Army Pershings entered combat near Tabu-dong with Co.C, 73rd Tank Battalion supporting the 27th Infantry Regiment. The North Koreans lost 13 T-34-85 tanks and five SU-76M assault guns to the Pershings and infantry in two savage days of fighting. By mid-August the NKPA 105th Tank Brigade was in poor shape. It was losing an increasing number of tanks to UN air attack, and the mechanical state of its vehicles was poor after two months of hard fighting. Furthermore, with tanks now becoming far more common on the UN side, the North Korean tankers could not assume that they could attack unopposed. The training of the NKPA tankers was adequate when facing demoralized infantry, but it was poor when compared to the US tankers. In many encounters with M26 Pershings, the NKPA would fire high-explosive projectiles which had been adequate against the M24 Light tanks, but against the thickly armored M26, these were ineffective. The T-34-85 tank was not armored well enough to resist the 90mm tank gun fire of the M26, and could be readily penetrated from normal combat ranges. As a result, most US tank losses during the Pusan perimeter fighting were due to encounters with mines or NKPA 45mm Model 1942 anti-tank guns. On the night of 27 August, the NKPA 105th Tank Brigade began its last major tank attack through the valley. This was preceded by heavy tracer fire between the hills, which led to its nickname, "the Bowling Alley."

By September the UN forces in the Pusan perimeter had gained numerical superiority over the NKPA forces with about 400 US Army and Marine Corps tanks facing only about 40 NKPA T-34-85 tanks. Instead of making a breakout from the Pusan perimeter, UN commander Gen Douglas MacArthur ordered an amphibious landing by X Corps behind

Some M26 tanks were upgraded to M26A1 standards by substituting the newer M3A1 90mm gun with its distinctive fume extractor and new muzzle brake. The latter is not evident in this view because of the canvas cover over the barrel. This is a Marine M26A1 near Hamhung, on the eastern coast of Korea, on November 10, 1950. Around this time it became the practice in some Marine units to paint the vehicle tactical number on the mantlet. (US National Archives)

The early production M46 used a distinctive cover over the rear muffler that did not extend down the sides as did the final production types. These M46 Patton tanks of the 64th Tank Battalion take up defensive positions at Kagae-dong in support of the 3rd Infantry Div. in an attempt to stem the tide of the Chinese advance on December 7, 1950. (US Army)

In one of the epic battles of the Korean War, the 5th and 7th Marines, trapped by Chinese forces near the Chosin reservoir, began an attack to break out of the encirclement. A column of M26A1 Pershings support the attack on December 6, 1950. *(US National Archives)*

the main NKPA forces at the port city of Inchon. By landing at Inchon, the UN forces would cut off the main NKPA forces besieging the Pusan perimeter. The Inchon landing on September 16, 1950, was conducted by 1st Marine Division, supported by 1st Marine Tank Battalion, followed by the US Army 7th Infantry Division and its 73rd Tank Battalion.

The NKPA forces near Inchon were weak, consisting mainly of new units raised and trained for deployment to the south. The Marine M26 Pershings were used predominantly to provide fire-support, but a number of tank skirmishes did occur. The NKPA's new 42nd Mechanized Regiment, equipped with 18 T-34-85 tanks, was deployed near Seoul. About half of these tried to counter-attack the landing area during the late afternoon of September 16. Three were quickly destroyed by air attack, and three more were destroyed in a short and one-sided duel with Marine M26 Pershings. The next morning, six T-34-85 tanks stumbled into the positions of the 5th Marines near Kimpo airfield. Before they could react, they were taken under fire by Marine recoilless rifles and by M26 Pershing tanks of the 1st Marine Tank Battalion. They were wiped out without loss to the Marines.

During the four days after the landings a total of 24 T-34-85 tanks were destroyed in combat, effectively eliminating the 42nd Mechanized Regiment. Another new unit in training, the 43rd Tank Regiment was sent into the fray on September 25, 1950, losing 12 T-34-85 tanks, of which seven were knocked out by Marine Pershings. The main role of the Pershings in the Seoul fighting was in providing close fire-support during urban combat, such as for destroying barricades which the NKPA had erected across the streets.

The success of the Inchon landing was followed by a break-out from the Pusan perimeter by the Eighth Army. With their lifelines to North Korea threatened by the landings, the NKPA forces were in a panic. The 105th Armored Brigade had already been ordered north to attack the Inchon beach-head, but the remaining NKPA forces were still in place when the counter-offensive began on 17 September. The NKPA was forced into a general retreat which resulted in an ignominious rout. What was left of the North Korean tank force was destroyed in the ensuing fighting in September and early October.

There were hardly any encounters with North Korean armor after November 1950. The US Army concluded that the M26 was a markedly more effective tank than the M4A3E8 Sherman in tank fighting, being about 3.5 times more effective in offensive missions and 3.05 times more effective overall.

Less than half of the tanks sent to Korea by the US in 1950 were M26 or M46. US tank units in

Korea received 1,326 tanks, including 309 M26 Pershings, 200 M46 Pattons, 679 M4A3E8 Shermans, and 138 M24 Chaffees. Three of the Army tank battalions were mixed M4A3E8/M26 units (70th, 72nd, and 89th Tank Bns.), one was an M26 battalion (73rd Heavy Tank Bn.) and two were M46 units (6th and 64th Tank Bns.). The Marines deployed a single M26 Tank battalion (Marine 1st Tank Bn.) and three M26 anti-tank platoons.

A study conducted after the war counted 119 tank-vs-tank actions during the war, 104 involving US Army tank units and 15 involving the Marine 1st Tank Bn. The M26 and M46 were involved in nearly half of these, the M26 in 38 actions (32 per cent), and the M46 in 12 actions (10 per cent). Only 24 of the 119 engagements involved more than three North Korean tanks and most were small-scale encounters of platoon size or less. The relatively small number of tank-vs-tank battles of the M46 was due to the fact that none saw combat until early September. A total of 34 US tanks were knocked out by North Korean armor, including 6 M26 and 8 M46 tanks, of which only 15 were totally lost. The US tanks knocked out 97 T-34-85 tanks and claimed a further 18 as probables. The M26 was credited with 39 per cent of the NKPA tank losses and the M46 12 per cent. About half of the engagements took place at ranges of 350 yards or less, and at this distance the M26 had a hit probability of 85 per cent, somewhat higher when firing HVAP and somewhat lower when firing APC ammunition. About 20 per cent of the engagements took place at 350–750 yards, and a similar number at 750–1,150 yards. Hit probabilities at these ranges were 69 per cent and 46 per cent respectively. These figures are comparable to the M46 and M4A3E8 Medium tanks, since at the time all US tanks had similar fire control systems. The shortest engagement range was 10 yards, and the longest known successful engagement by an M26 is 3,000 yards.

The intervention of the Chinese Peoples Liberation Army (PLA) in November changed the course of the war. Following the dramatic UN advance to the Chinese frontier in the fall of 1950, there was an equally precipitous retreat to the 38th Parallel. The M26 and M46 fought in many of these battles, some M26 tanks of the 1st Marine Tank Bn. supporting the Marines during the legendary withdrawal from the

After the withdrawal from the Chosin reservoir, the Marine 1st Tank Battalion remained in eastern Korea, ferreting out North Korean stragglers who had escaped into the hills the previous fall. The crews fire their .50 cal machine guns on M26A1 and M4A3 (105) tanks at enemy forces in the hills.
(US National Archives)

Chosin reservoir. By the end of 1950 Seoul had fallen again and the UN forces had been pushed back to the Han River. In mid-January 1951 the Eighth Army had 670 tanks, including 50 M26 and M26A1 Pershings and 97 M46 Pattons, which took part in the ensuing counter-offensive. By April 1951 the UN forces had pushed the Chinese back to the 38th Parallel, where the war had started, and the two sides settled into a protracted and bloody stalemate.

Although the US Army had found its tank units very valuable in both the offensive and defensive phases of the war, there was a conviction among the senior leadership in Washington that tanks were not necessary in the mountainous terrain along the 38th Parallel. No further tank battalions were deployed, and new types such as the M47 tank and M41 Light tank were not deployed in Korea. The mobile phase of the Korean War had ended. It was replaced by a "war of the outposts" as local efforts were made by both sides to eliminate key defensive positions of the opposing force. Tanks continued to be used at the end of the war in 1953 to support the infantry, most often in direct fire-support missions or to supplement conventional artillery. They were valuable because their guns could be used to destroy enemy bunkers at long ranges across valleys and ridges. Special tank roads and tank entrenchments were created so the tanks could move rapidly from sector to sector to where they were most needed; however, between 1951 and 1953 Korea was mainly an infantry and artillery war.

One innovation adopted on the M46 during the war was the use of a large searchlight for night fire-support missions. These 18in. diameter lights were mounted above the main gun and deployed in some numbers in 1952. Experiments were also conducted, under the codename "Leaflet II" on the use of infra-red searchlights, but these were not deployed.

The opinion of US tankers towards the various types of US tanks changed in 1951 once the T-34-85 threat disappeared. Although the M26 had been popular in the summer of 1950, when its armor and firepower had been so desperately needed, opinions soured as its mechanical

unreliability became more evident. At the heart of the problem was its engine, which was the same as that of the M4A3E8 tank. In the mountainous terrain of Korea, with the enemy tank threat gone, many tank battalions preferred the more reliable M4A3E8. The M46 cured many of the problems encountered with the M26 by the introduction of a new engine and cross-drive transmission, and so was preferred over the M26, but a post-war study concluded that the ideal tank would have been a vehicle with the armor and firepower of the M26 and M46 and the automotive reliability of the M4A3E8 Sherman.

The M26 had been declared "limited standard" before the outbreak of the Korean War and was retired from service shortly after. The M46 and M46A1 were declared obsolete in February 1957 and were retired from service due to the advent of more modern members of the Patton family, the M47 and M48.

Marine M26 Pershing tanks of Co.C, Marine 1st Tank Battalion supported by a single M4A3 (105mm) howitzer tank provide fire-support during the second phase of Operation Ripper, near Hongchon, on March 14, 1951, during attempts to reach the 38th Parallel. (US National Archives)

THE M26 AND M46 IN FOREIGN SERVICE

Neither the M26 nor the M46 were widely exported compared to other wartime US tanks, and during World War II a single T26E3 was delivered to Britain for trials. In the late 1940s the US Army began transferring tanks to allies in Europe as part of an effort to build up their forces against the Soviet Union and its allies, but these were mostly M4 Sherman tanks. Due to the outbreak of the war in Korea, M26 and M46 tanks were at a premium, putting a limit on transfers to the new NATO armies. Following the Korean War and the reinvigoration of the US tank industry, the improved M47 Patton became the preferred tank for export. As a result, some European armies received small numbers of M26 or M46 to acquaint them with the Patton tank series, but only

France, Belgium, and Italy received significant numbers. France received the M26, but principally relied on the later M47 Patton until its own AMX-30 tank emerged in the late 1960s. Italy was provided with the M26, which served with the Ariete Brigade (later a division) in the early 1950s. Belgium received a batch of M26 tanks in 1951, which served in both the regular tank battalions and in reserve armor units. In 1952 Belgium received eight M46A1 Pattons for use at the Leopoldsburg tank training center for transition training of Sherman tank crews to the new M47. Although there were plans to supply Pershings to other NATO armies, the shortages of vehicles caused by the Korean War led the US to fund the purchase of British Centurion tanks for both the Netherlands and Denmark.

China captured a number of M26 and M46 tanks during the Korean War. At least one of these is preserved in the army museum in Beijing, and China turned over a few to the Soviet Union in the early 1950s for test and evaluation – one of which survives in the armor museum at Kubinka. A curious offshoot of this exchange was the subsequent use of bore evacuators on Soviet tanks. This stemmed from the inspection of the M3A1 90mm gun on the M26A1 and M46 tanks. Amazingly enough, one of the T26E3s which fought with the 9th Armored Division at Remagen was found on an Air Force target range decades later and after restoration is displayed at the Wright Museum in Wolfesboro, New Hampshire.

The M26 Pershing was supplied in small numbers to several NATO armies. These French Pershings are on patrol near Rastatt, along the Rhine River, on April 9, 1953, in the French occupation zone in Germany. (US Army)

THE PLATES

PLATE A:
T26E3 PERSHING, CO.B, 19TH TANK BATTALION, 9TH ARMORED DIVISION, REMAGEN, GERMANY, MARCH 1945

The Pershing tanks of the Zebra Mission were very simply marked when they first went into combat. Aside from the normal Allied white stars on the turret side, glacis plate, and engine deck, markings were confined mostly to shipping stencils painted on the side skirts. The tank registration number is painted in yellow on the ventilation hump between the driver and co-driver stations. The white stencil towards the rear of the side skirt (HAIL-AA-ORDII-SO-5H300L051) is a shipping code, while the other blocks of stencils are shipping information regarding the size and volume of the tank, the status of anti-freeze, and other details. The warning "LIFT HERE" was stenciled near the four tank lift rings to assist the dock crane crews to position lifting hooks properly. Curiously enough, none of the usual US Army unit bumper codes was carried.

PLATE B:
T26E1 SUPER PERSHING, 33RD ARMORED REGIMENT, 3RD ARMORED DIVISION, GERMANY, MARCH 1945

On arriving in Germany, the 3rd Armored Division ordnance personnel put additional applique armor on the bow and turret front and later added some "Mickey Mouse ears" of laminate armor plate to protect the turret front corners. The

A gaudy M46 Patton of the US Army 6th Tank Battalion helps extract another M46 from a muddy rice paddy near Chongpyong on April 2, 1951. These colorful tiger markings remained in use until later in the spring, by which time they had become scruffy. They were overpainted during periodic overhaul. (US Army)

A Marine unit moves past an M26A1 of the 1st Tank Battalion. The column is led by an M29 81mm mortar team, with the lead marine carrying the bipod, followed by the tube and then the baseplate. (US National Archives)

The Marine 1st Tank Battalion had been re-equipped with M46 Patton tanks after the spring 1951 campaign, to make up for its losses. Here, Co.A re-arms for a fire mission on April 25, 1952, in western Korea, south of Panmunjom, near the Jamestown Line. The 90mm ammunition was delivered in two-round wooden crates, while the rounds themselves were stored in black fiberboard tubes for added protection. (US National Archives)

vehicle was camouflage painted, with bands of black sprayed over the usual olive drab. Markings were simple. The vehicle tactical number A 2 was crudely painted on the turret applique armor. On the lower lip of the bow applique armor was the usual assortment of unit bumper codes, with the registration number in the center 3^33^ 30103292 II.

PLATE C1:
M26 PERSHING, CO.B, MARINE 1ST TANK BATTALION, INCHON, KOREA, SEPTEMBER 1950
The Marine Pershings were delivered in normal Army colors and share the standard olive drab finish. The vehicle carries Marine tactical markings in yellow, which indicates the company, platoon, and individual vehicle. The TK<2> marking is the temporary divisional insignia with embarkation number painted on it preceded by TK, for the 1st Tank Battalion. On the stowage pannier USMC has overpainted the Army registration number, though the last digits – 118039 – are still evident. There are white markings chalked on the front side skirt, probably shipping markings. Although Marines tanks did not regularly carry the US Army's white star insignia during the Korean War, the tanks fighting at Inchon did usually carry them.

PLATE C2:
M26 PERSHING, ARIETE ARMORED DIVISION, NATO "SALDATURA VENETA" WARGAME, FRUILI, ITALY, AUGUST 1963
This Italian Pershing is finished in olive drab with a large white X wargame marking. Italian Pershings were often simply marked with insignia consisting of a white registration box on the bow and stern with the registration number in black, preceded by the national tricolor.

PLATE D: (CROSS-SECTIONAL DRAWING)
M26 PERSHING TANK, US ARMY 1945
The Pershing underwent modifications in the light of experiences of the Zebra Mission, including the addition of reinforcements for the fenders. This cutaway shows the typical coloring of US tanks of the period: lusterless olive drab exterior and gloss white interiors. Some of the interior parts were painted in colors other than white, generally items that were GFE (Government furnished equipment) that was supplied to the manufacturer from government stocks.

PLATE E:
M46 PATTON, CO.C, 6TH TANK BATTALION, HAN RIVER, FEBRUARY 1951
During the winter 1950–51 campaign, American tankers began painting garish tiger faces on their tanks, believing that they would terrify superstitious Chinese peasant soldiers. This led to some of the most colorful tank combat markings

of all time, and the 6th Tank Battalion markings stand out as being particularly gaudy. The turret and parts of the hull were painted in yellow, with stripes and detail in black, white, and red. The bumper codes on this tank are 8A 6^ C-3.

The tanks in the unit often carried the vehicle tactical number in white on the turret side, and the eight-digit vehicle registration number was left on a patch of olive drab on the side stowage box. M46 registration numbers ran in a series from 30162866 to 30163664.

PLATE F1:
M46 PATTON, CO.A, 73RD TANK BATTALION, HAN RIVER, FEBRUARY 1951
Some of the M46 Patton tanks of the 73rd Tank Battalion were painted with this colorful tiger marking in February/March 1951 during the fighting along the Han River. The fenders were painted to resemble the tiger's claws and paws, and the details differed from tank to tank. The vehicle bumper codes were painted immediately below the drivers'

ABOVE **The Chinese often launched massed infantry attacks at night in the hope of reducing their losses to US defenses. As a result, US tanks began to be equipped with 18in. General Electric searchlights in the summer of 1952. This is an M46 Patton of Co.C, Marine 1st Tank Battalion on August 27, 1952. (US National Archives)**

BELOW **In contrast to the summer and fall of 1950, where tank-vs-tank fighting was frequent, in later years US tanks were used primarily to provide direct artillery fire-support. This Marine M46 of Co.A, 1st Marine Tank Battalion waits for fire instructions on December 15, 1952, while supporting the Commonwealth Division to the east. A large number of fused high-explosive rounds wait behind the tank for a possible fire mission. (US National Archives)**

hatches, as they often became covered with mud if painted in the usual location at the junction of the two hull plates. The vehicle unit bumper codes on this tank, nicknamed TAIL SPIN are 73^ A-35. This tank also had a standard 20in. white star on either side of the turret, and would have had a large white star painted on the engine deck.

PLATE F2:
M46 PATTON, 64TH TANK BATTALION, HAN RIVER, FEBRUARY 1951

The 64th Tank Battalion was a mixed formation of M4A3E8 and M26/M46 tanks and supported the 3rd Infantry Division. The tiger's head insignia on this tank is painted over the shoulder patch insignia of the 3rd Infantry Division, which is a blue and white diagonally-striped square. The actual faces on each of the M4A3E8s and M46s of the battalion differed from vehicle to vehicle; some were rather badly proportioned, like this one here, looking more like a wolf than a tiger.

PLATE G:
M46 PATTON, CO.C, MARINE 1ST TANK BATTALION, KOREA, 1952

The Marine 1st Tank Battalion had relatively standard markings for most of the Korean War. The vehicle tactical number beginning with the company number was painted on the turret in white, as seen here, or sometimes in yellow. By 1952 the practice was to paint USMC with the Marine globe and anchor insignia on the ventilation bulge between the driver and co-driver stations. The US Army white star marking was generally not carried at this stage of the war. This tank is one of those fitted with the new General Electric searchlight for night fighting.

Chinese troops did not have an adequate infantry anti-tank weapon during the Korean War but did use captured US bazookas. During the outpost fighting in 1952/53, Chinese troops would infiltrate UN lines to attack entrenched UN tanks, so this Marine dozer M46 is fitted with an improvised anti-bazooka screen made from chain-link fence, on March 25, 1953. (US National Archives)

In 1953 some Marine M46 Patton tanks had improvised baskets mounted on the left side of the turret near the loader's hatch. These were to catch the spent brass ammunition casings. So much ammunition was expended during artillery fire missions that the basket was more convenient than having to police up the area for spent casings after each fire mission. (US National Archives)

INDEX

Figures in **bold** refer to illustrations